Traveling St. Pete 🦆 A Girls Guide

Melanie Bowman and Meredith Gaunce

Illustrations by Erin Salzer Hanna

Published by St. Petersburg Press
St. Petersburg, FL

Illustrations by Erin Salzer Hanna

Design and composition by St. Petersburg Press

Cover and interior design by St. Petersburg Press and Pablo Guidi

ISBN: 9781940300245

First Edition

Traveling St. Pete 🦆 A Girls Guide

Melanie Bowman and Meredith Gaunce

Illustrations by Erin Salzer Hanna

Congratulations! You either live in the best city in the country or you made the wise decision to come visit her. We hope you find this guidebook to be helpful in finding some of St. Pete's gems and planning your vacation or staycation.

We had to be selective with our featured sites, so this is by no means exhaustive of all St. Pete has to offer. We only included spots that have been open for two years or more, since restaurants and shops – even the ones we find most fabulous – tend to alter their hours, relocate or even close (gasp) so be sure to double-check websites or social media to find the most current information. Since St. Pete is a city best celebrated outdoors, all of the food and drinks featured can be enjoyed outside.

Also, we want you to know that these are our honest, non-influenced favorites. We did not allow any venues to "purchase" a spot in our book. However, some places may be so stoked to be selected that they will offer a discount if you bring the book with you when you go!

This book would not have been possible without the support of our husbands (thank you, Jon, Jesse and Andy!), the amazing illustrations, the help of our publisher St. Petersburg Press and the input from our friends (we love you and owe you a Kahwa*, Elizabeth, Amanda, Laura Jo, Rachel & Ashley).

Enjoy St. Pete!
Xo,
Mel & Mer

*To many in St. Pete, a Kahwa = a coffee.

Table of Contents

RESTAURANTS

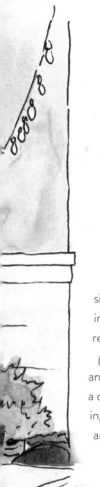

ANNATA

300 BEACH DRIVE N.E. / 727-851-9582
ANNATAWINE.COM

If the weather cooperates, sit outside, because Annata is situated right on Beach Drive, one of the must-stroll streets in downtown St. Pete. It is a great place to people watch and really feel the city. They do not take reservations and tend to get busy, but here is what you do: Put your name on the list and walk a few doors down to the Canopy rooftop bar to grab a drink while you wait for your table. Annata has an outstanding wine list and the menu consists of charcuterie, flatbreads, and pastas (homemade of course), and the menu lends itself perfectly to sharing mutliple dishes amongst friends.

BELLA BRAVA

204 BEACH DRIVE N.E. / (727) 895-5515
BELLABRAVA.COM

BB is relatively old school St. Pete (opened in 2005), centrally located in the heart of downtown on Beach Drive. If the weather cooperates, it's the perfect spot to watch the city while drinking from a fantastic wine selection, eating woodfired pizzas and pastas. It's directly across from the pier, so you could easily take a pier walk before or after dinner or peruse the shops on Beach Drive. I love their goat cheese appetizer, but really you cannot go wrong.

BODEGA

—

1120 CENTRAL AVENUE / 727-623-0942
EATATBODEGA.COM

No frills and Latin inspired, this place always delivers what it promises, delicious food! It's bold and colorful building matches the bold flavors of their sandwiches, platos and juices. You can expect to wait at least (but probably more than) 15 minutes for your food, but order a Cuban coffee to enjoy while you wait. You won't find a more authentic Cuban coffee or sandwich in St. Pete and pork lovers rave about the lechon plate again and again. I love taking the pollo asado sandwich to Green Bench Brewing Co. next door and getting a cider. Read "Mel's favorite day in St. Pete".

BRICK & MORTAR

539 CENTRAL AVENUE / 727-822-6540

Despite not having much of a website or online presence
(sorry, B & M folks, but it's true), this is the real deal. They
make a cioppino that is out of this world, and if you like
octopus, they often do an octopus three-ways dish that is
one of my all-time favorite dishes ever. It's upscale, but not
stuffy, and as is true with basically everywhere in St. Pete, you
can wear jeans, shorts, or a dress. Welcome to the city where
anything goes!

CAPPY'S

2900 1ST AVENUE N. / 727-321-3020
CAPPYSPIZZAONLINE.COM

Hands-down the best pizza in the city! There are a few
Cappy's locations now, but the St. Pete location is the OG.
The menus are old album covers, and there are Trivial Pursuit
cards on the tables. Literally the only things offered are pizza,
calzones and salad, but they are all perfection. Enter Cappy's
charming bungalow and write your name and party size on
a chalkboard when you walk in. A quintessential St. Pete
neighborhood spot, Cappy's is perfect if you are looking for a
casual spot to get a pizza and beer. However, be warned that
they have been in an epic parking lot battle with the ballet
studio next door. Check the parking signs carefully if you drive
there or risk being pummeled by militant dancers.

Cassis

170 BEACH DRIVE / 727-827-2927
CASSISSTPETE.COM

A French inspired bakery, this is a great people watching spot with plenty of outdoor seating. They make no apologies for their pricey food and drinks, and when you taste any one of their benedicts (all amazing) you will likely agree that it's worth it. The lemon ricotta blueberry pancakes are my go-to. If you don't have time for a sit down brunch or breakfast, (or if you have room for a snack) you can grab a pastry or any one of the delicious artisan desserts from the bakery. Take your French treat and walk along the waterfront or window shop on Beach Drive.

DATZ

180 CENTRAL AVENUE / 727-202-1182
DATZTAMPA.COM

With a happy and carefree vibe, this restaurant is known for its comfort food on steroids that will leave you and your girlfriends with lots of Instagram worthy pics of food and drink. The portions are huge, the drinks are poured generously. Your blood sugar will spike just by looking at the Monkey Bread, but go for it, you won't be sorry, and you will likely appreciate their excellent Weekday Happy Hour Menu.

HAWKER'S

1235 CENTRAL AVENUE / 727-521-7253
EATHAWKERS.COM

Never underestimate the power of Asian comfort food. The
vibe in Hawker's is energetic, accessible, hip, yet family (and
big group) friendly. The Crispy Tofu Bites, Beef Haw Fun,
the Shrimp and Papaya Salad, the Roti Kanai (flatbread with
curry dipping sauce), and Po Po Lo's Curry are my favorites.
Good things happen here! This is where Mel and Mer met for
the first time and the excitement to write this book was born!
Even though it is not exclusive to St. Pete, it holds a special
place in our hearts for this reason alone. And it is delicious.

IL RITORNO

449 CENTRAL AVENUE / 727-897-5900
ILRITORNODOWNTOWN.COM

A self-proclaimed "Modern Italian Eatery," Il Ritorno is a local St. Petersburg gem. Think elegant but not pretentious. Think fine dining and also jeans, because anything goes at Il Ritorno. The pasta is made from scratch, the fish is always fresh, and the greens delectable. When you take a bite of the Short Rib Mezzaluna, you taste the labor of love that goes into each dish. The award-winning chef, David Benstock, is known for his commitment to fresh ingredients, so the menu is seasonal and always changing. The talent at Il Ritorno expanded their gifts to offerings such as St. Pete Meat & Provisions, a great place to stock up on goods for your outdoor picnic.

LEFT BANK BISTRO

—

1225 DR. MARTIN LUTHER KING JR. STREET N. /
727-256-1691
THELEFTBANKBISTRO.COM

Left Bank is one of the newer restaurants on our list of faves. I've never been to Paris (hint hint, husband) but this is what I picture. The owner did an incredible job keeping the charm of the 1920's home that houses the restaurant, and the Chef created a menu that uses mostly local ingredients in his spin on traditional French dishes. This is a bold statement, but I firmly believe that their Potato Crusted Snapper is the best fish dish in the city. There is a champagne-citrus beurre blanc on the plate that I wish I could bottle, keep in my purse and drizzle on everything I eat. Sit on the patio and I promise you will feel like you are in St. Pete's version of Paris.

LOLITA'S WINE MARKET

16 18TH STREET S. / 727-505-0503
LOLITASWINEMARKET.COM

I don't think it's too extreme to say this is my favorite restaurant in St. Pete. I will be going here for my birthday, my anniversary, my best friend's birthday, my mom's birthday- you get the point. I get the meatballs every time and I'm a sucker for their amazing wine list. It is sadly not super easy for large parties to get seated in this small, but beautiful and eclectic, space. For the larger party who still wants to experience Lolita's, you can take your create-your-own charcuterie board, affordable and delicious wines, and small plates to go. They will give you your meal in a cute pizza box and you can enjoy your meat and cheese board at the park, or any of the beautiful green spaces St. Pete has to offer.

NITALLY'S

1163 MARTIN LUTHER KING JR. STREET N.
/ 727-290-6166 THAIMEX.CO

I ♥ ST. PET

If a Mexican restaurant and Thai restaurant fell in love and had a baby, its name would be Nitally's. This place is known for its delicious food, but not its service. Don't sweat the slower than usual wait time. Everything is being made from scratch and to order. While you wait, indulge in the delicious red sangria that is only for the cinnamon lover and then when your orange chicken tacos, my absolute favorite, arrive, you will understand what the fuss is all about. The Panang Mole and the Pad Thai dishes are what put Nitally's on the map. You may want to request no spice. Really, sometimes the mild is too much. The spice situation at Nitally's is not for the faint of heart. You have been warned.

PACIFIC COUNTER

660 CENTRAL AVENUE / 727-440-7008
PACIFICCOUNTER.COM

It is impossible to not smile and be drawn in when you see the pink facade of Pacific Counter. This is the perfect spot to pick up a make-your-own Hawaiian-inspired bowl with fresh veggies and seafood and take it outside for a picnic in our abundant waterfront greenspace - oooh, or even the Pier! Did you know that Pacific Counter doesn't waste any food? They find ways to donate the food while it is still fresh to local places who need it most. We love them for their picture-perfect dishes, sensational flavor combinations and most of all, the energy they bring to St. Pete.

Red Mesa Cantina

128 3rd Street S. / 855-265-0812
REDMESACANTINA.COM

A family owned and operated Mexican restaurant, Red Mesa Cantina is a longstanding favorite for many St. Pete locals. They have a calming courtyard with a waterfall outside, or you can sit inside and enjoy the beautiful and vibrant ambiance which includes one of the two bars that boasts a very impressive tequila selection and also delightful sangria. The filet mignon tacos, the crab and shrimp quesadillas, and the seafood mofongo are consistently good. Share almost any small plate, you can't go wrong, but not before trying the yummy (and very fresh) guacamole!

THE LIBRARY

600 5TH STREET S. / 727-369-9969
THELIBRARYSTPETE.COM

I totally get your apprehension about the Library being in the base of a hospital building, but trust me when I say that other than seeing lots of people eating in scrubs, you would have no idea this trendy gem was on a hospital campus. The walls are mostly filled with books - hence the name - but with these grand high ceilings, it doesn't feel like a library. For an appetizer, they have these Fried Brussel Sprouts that are the perfect amount of spicy and not too fried. It is excellent for brunch (available Saturday and Sunday) with sweet and savory things perfect for sharing. My fave is the Lemon Poppy French Toast.

TROPHY FISH

2060 CENTRAL AVENUE / 727-258-7883
TROPHYFISHSTPETE.COM

"Ahoy Captain," is what I feel like saying every time I walk into Trophy Fish. The fish here has literally been caught that day! I can picture the fisherman reeling in my about-to-be meal and I want to personally thank them for their hard work. Does that sound strange? They say to "come early and come hungry" and they aren't kidding! They only serve what they catch and sometimes they do run out of fish, hence their no reservation policy. My favorite appetizer here is the smoked fish spread without the jalapeño. My go-to mains are the fish tacos or the fish plate. I highly recommend the "If you like Piña Colada" if you're in the mood for a boat drink, and let's be honest, if you're at Trophy Fish you're in the mood for a boat drink! Go for it, you're on vacation. Jimmy Buffett would be so proud.

SHOPPING

ASHE COUTURE

1027 CENTRAL AVENUE / (727) 828-9925
ASHECOUTURE.COM

If you like brands like Billabong and Free People, this is the store for you. It kind of has a surfer girl feel, and if you enjoy fashion, you need to check it out. If you forgot your swimsuit or just want another, they usually have an incredible swimsuit collection, and their cover-ups are the kind that make you feel famous. You know the kind. They flow behind you, and you kind of walk in slow motion with your own personal life soundtrack playing some bada$$ music. Yup, those.

CANVAS FASHION GALLERY

1535 4TH STREET N. / 727-317-5572
SHOPCFG.COM

This store somehow oozes confidence that rubs off on its shoppers. The stuff I have bought here just makes me feel good. The clothes, jewelry, art and shoes are for the à la mode girl who wants to feel a little bit sassy. Changing their merchandise all the time, this store knows how to keep its patrons interested (and fashionable) all year long and for any occasion.

FLORIDA CRAFT ART

501 Central Avenue / 727-821-7391
FLORIDACRAFTART.ORG

This huge space feels like all the really expensive things on
Etsy got together and decided to have a parade to show
off how beautiful they are. Everything is handmade, classy,
sophisticated, yet the pricing is thoughtful and (mostly)
attainable. One of my favorite local artists, Blossom and Shine
(thank you B&S for my favorite bracelet, I'm still wearing it!)
is upstairs in The ArtLofts, where local artists rent space to
create and sell their art.

MARION'S

1301 4TH STREET N. / 727-821-2345
MARIONS4THSTREET.COM

A quintessential St. Pete establishment, this charming
boutique has been around for more than three decades,
and once you go there you will understand why. In every
nook and cranny they have curated a beautiful display of art,
jewelry, handbags, clothes, stationery, home decor, kitchen
gadgets, books, kids toys, and much more. There is something
for everyone here - every budget, every age. The staff lives
up to its hospitable and kind reputation every time and Mr.
Cooper, the official greeter (the store manager's chocolate lab
furbaby) may or may not meet you at the door to give a warm
hello. Not to be forgotten is the free gift wrapping, which
is lovely and so appreciated, especially if you're traveling.
Located just a couple miles north of downtown you'll want to
plan to take a car.

MISRED OUTFITTERS

615 CENTRAL AVENUE / 727-827-8310
BEMISRED.COM

I challenge you to walk into Misred and not buy something.
The price point is perfect for grabbing a cute dress to wear on
vacay or shoes if the ones you brought turned out to be much
less comfortable than they were in your mind. Another cool
thing about Misred is they had so many fabulous accessories
that they took over the storefront next door and have an
entire store dedicated to affordable accessories.

PLAIN JANE

621 CENTRAL AVENUE / 727-600-7741
PLAINJANESTPETE.COM

I'll just go ahead and admit that I am pretty sure I am Plain Jane's #1 fan. If you like Anthropologie, you will love Plain Jane. It is smaller than Anthro (yeah, we are on a nickname basis) but carries a lot of the same brands - Cloth and Stone, Johnny Was, Sanctuary - and Karen, the owner, does such a great job having gems for all price points. Need an adorable tote to walk around town with a map of the city on it? Go to Plain Jane. Need a shirt/hat/trinket with St. Pete on it? Go to Plain Jane. Need a gift for your friend taking care of your dog? Go to Plain Jane. Need a beautiful shirt or dress to remember how much you love shopping in St. Pete? Go to Plain Jane. You're welcome.

SATURDAY MORNING MARKET

100 1ST STREET S.E. / (727) 455-4921
SATURDAYMORNINGMARKET.COM

If you are visiting St. Pete on a weekend between October and May, you need to put the SMM on your Saturday to-do list. Think about the market as a treasure trove of the best St. Pete highlights put on display in one place. This market, which claims to be the biggest in the southeast, includes 170+ vendors that will impress your senses with organic and local food of any kind, live music, art, crafts, and lots of shopping. The friendly and lively vibe of the market is top notch and reflects the unique and highest expression of the very beautiful Sunshine City. Allow yourself at least an hour, (but probably more) to really experience the market.

Spas and Pampering

NOUVELLE

—

475 CENTRAL AVE #101 / 727-896-2700
NOUVELLEBEAUTYBAR.COM

If you didn't make it to your pre-vacay mani/pedi, call (or walk in to) Nouvelle! Ideal for groups, Nouvelle is worlds above your strip mall nail salon. Andrea is likely working the bar, and you can even order snacks or lunch from La V - the best Vietnamese restaurant in the city - to be delivered to you while you are receiving your service. Not. Even. Kidding. At the corner of Central Avenue and 5th Street, you are right in the middle of everything to walk a bit and let your nails dry.

Pia's Day Spa

1900 Dr. Martin Luther King Jr. Street N.
727-346-6740
BYPIA.COM

Just a few miles outside of downtown Pia's is nestled in a historic residential neighborhood. They offer spa services in a charming one-hundred-year-old home that will make you feel...well...at home. They offer everything from manicures to microblading, but if you have to pick one service, ask for Nayla (the owner) or Rachel to give you a massage. "I don't have time for a massage on vacation," said no one ever.

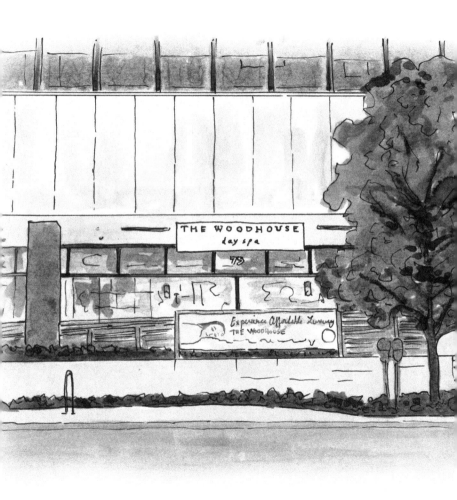

THE WOODHOUSE DAY SPA

75 1st Street S. / 727-228-1646
STPETE.WOODHOUSESPAS.COM

Have you ever been to a spa where you are so relaxed in your cozy robe, drinking your champagne that you kind of forget where you are? The Woodhouse is totally that place. Is the ultimate spa experience where the services are perfect, relaxation is guaranteed, and you walk out feeling like a different woman. There's a room where you lounge in your comfy robe and drink tea or champagne between services that is right out of HGTV - beautifully decorated, gorgeous light fixtures, and little tucked-away areas perfect for you and a couple of your closest girlfriends.

Snacks and Drinks

CRAFT KAFE

Thank goodness there are two of them now! We used to have to trek across the city to enjoy their quiches and pastries, but now there is one on Central Avenue in the heart of downtown. If you have any dietary restrictions or just like vegan options, this is the best place to go! I get so pumped when people suggest business coffee meetings there, because it means I get to have the most amazing apple cinnamon muffin! Oh, and of course I am super stoked to be having coffee with you, business contact.

Hyppo Popsicles

627 Central Avenue / 727-498-6536
THEHYPPO.COM

It's possible we had my son's birthday here. Twice. Hyppo makes gourmet popsicles and started here in Florida. They now have multiple locations and sell their pops in local Publix stores (Publixes? Publi?). They are constantly coming up with new flavors and at any given time have around 30 to choose from. My favorites are the Champagne Mango, Cherry Key Lime and Tangerine Cream. You can have any flavor dipped in chocolate, and I silently judge people who do not select that option. It is literally the perfect snack to help beat the Florida heat, and I am pretty sure it's healthy because it's made of fruit.

KAHWA COFFEE

—

475 2ND STREET N. *MULTIPLE LOCATIONS*
727-823-4700
KAHWACOFFEE.COM

I gotta hand it to the couple who is responsible for creating Kahwa, one of the most successful local coffee shops in town. They trailblazed their way all over town and took names. If you ask a local, they'll tell you that Kahwa is the new (way better) Starbucks. The gluten free muffins and almond milk lattés are a hit amongst the local crowd. If you go to the 2nd Avenue S. and 2nd Street location you're only a few blocks from the waterfront. Grab a buttery croissant and enjoy St. Petersburg's peaceful waterfront where it is not uncommon to see manatees, sea turtles, sting rays and even dolphins.

MAZZARO'S

2909 22ND AVENUE N. / 727-321-2400
MAZZAROSMARKET.COM

They take their food, wine, deli meats, cheeses, and coffee very seriously here and it pays off. This Italian Market is truly a destination and you can easily spend hours here. Start at the coffee bar late morning, relax while chatting or reading a book and then stay for lunch. You can grab a bottle of wine and something from the prepared foods selection or the deli (everything is delicious) and sit outside on the patio. Linger over your bottle of wine for hours and Italian treats before you try a homemade dessert from the bakery.

Paciugo Gelato

300 Beach Drive N.E., #120 / 727-209-0298
PACIUGOSTPETE.COM

This is my favorite place to night cap. There is something for everyone in your party - no matter how old or picky of an eater. My daughters deeply appreciate (and go crazy for) the Paciunicorn™, which claims native status to this gelato café. The chocolate-chocolate chip is a no brainer. The line for your gelato may be long but it is usually fast moving and it's totally worth it.

SWAH-REY

625 CENTRAL AVENUE / 727-767-0527
SWAH-REY.COM

Confession: I have never tried anything except the cupcakes. I
see they have these super creative cupcake shot things ("hook-
ups") and fancy cakes and coffee drinks (Kahwa coffee, of course),
but the cupcakes are mini and bitesize and amazing, so I can't
bring myself to venture out of my super delicious comfort zone.
They have about 20 different kinds, and I think I have had them
all (judgment free zone here, friends), but my favorites are the
cinnamon roll, pumpkin (seasonal), lemon and cookies & cream.

THE CANOPY

340 BEACH DRIVE N.E. / 727-896-1080
THEBIRCHWOOD.COM

This rooftop bar is the perfect place to pre-game while taking in the last glimpse of the beautiful Florida sunshine. We are the Sunshine City after all. They have private cabanas where you and your girlfriends can enjoy your craft cocktail and recap the day. I love coming here before I walk next door to Alto Mare or Annata Wine Bar for dinner. The Canopy is best experienced while its light out so you can really enjoy the views of downtown.

THE VINOY

501 5TH AVENUE N.E. / 727-894-1000
WWW.MARRIOTT.COM/HOTELS/TRAVEL/TPASR-THE-VINOY-
RENAISSANCE-ST-PETERSBURG-RESORT-AND-GOLF-CLUB

Many call the Vinoy the "heart" of downtown. This hotel is a throwback to Old Florida emanating 1920's art deco vibes. Whether you're a guest at The Vinoy or simply want to enjoy its history, make sure to spend time on the veranda. This is my favorite spot in St. Pete to have a drink on a lazy afternoon. Bonus points if you catch the casual and low key vibes of the Friday night live music session, also on the veranda. Paul's Landing, an American Cuisine restaurant, is ideal for a big group that wants to sit outside on a beautiful day. If you're feeling a little boujee, Marchand's has a fancy Sunday brunch that is only worth the cost if you love seafood. No matter how you experience this hotel, a trip to St. Pete is not complete without a visit to the Vinoy.

Urban Creamery

689 Central Avenue / 727-895-5953
URBANCREAMERYSTPETE.COM

Ice cream lovers rejoice! Urban Creamery has you covered for when you need an ice cream or Belgian waffle fix. The build-your-own concept (with toppings and sauces) allows for creativity and satisfaction all at the same time. While they do skillfully maneuver large crowds in this small space, I prefer to take my ice cream and scout out the night time vibe of downtown. Also, you can show off your masterpiece of a dessert while you walk. It's a thing.

MUSEUMS

THE DALI

When you see the building with huge glass bubbles coming out of it, you're in the right place! There's no use trying to resist the dreamlike state you are sure to experience here. It's a little trippy here, which is likely intentional given the artist's style. "The Persistence of Memory," arguably the most famous piece of surreal art in the world, lives here and never loses its appeal. Dali was one of the most brilliant surreal artists of all time and this beautiful and new(ish) museum is the perfect place to showcase his talent. With a permanent collection as well as visiting exhibits, The Dali never gets old.

Museum of Fine Art

Small but mighty, the permanent collection here leads the St. Pete art scene in diversity. There is something here for the art enthusiast and cynic alike. Visiting exhibits are usually top notch and frequently changing, so make sure to check out their website during your visit. If you spend too much time perusing art and get hungry, consider checking out the café which is in a prime location on the waterfront and serves great food.

The James Museum

This is a fairly new museum (opened in 2018) and is devoted solely to western and wildlife art. The most incredible part - other than the size (literally thousands of pieces) - is that this is the personal collection of Tom James (a well-known and respected local) and is only a fraction of it. Because there is more available, the exhibits are always changing and rotating. You can't miss the building - it is sleek, modern and has a giant bronze sculpture of a Native American man catching an eagle with his bare hands.

Imagine

All about glass, and how it is used to create beautiful things, Imagine is a stunning wonder that will leave you with a deep appreciation for this precious material that you never knew you needed more of. The geometric globe piece that you can stare into for hours and a display of over 1,000 Buddhas' heads are two of my favorites. Imagine, along with the Chihuly collection, is responsible for glass artists all over the world recognizing our area as a pioneer of the glass movement and some have even begun referring to the west coast of Florida, the "glass coast." Go see this glass!

The coolest thing to note about our museum scene is that there are too many incredible ones to list and St. Pete is one of the few places where new museums are continuing to open, so stay on your toes. We would be remiss if we did not mention the Florida Holocaust Museum located in central downtown. It is breathtaking and moving and a must-see.

BREWERIES

Whether you are a beer-lover, just beginning to learn about beer, or usually say "no thanks y'all" when it comes to beer, I strongly encourage you to consider exploring the St. Pete beer scene. The St. Pete tourist is diverse, discerning, smart and unique. The leaders of the local beer industry deeply understand that in order to stay in business, they have to constantly innovate, research, and cater to a very distinct and constantly changing consumer, including you, women! Therefore, go enjoy some brews ladies!

GreenBench

Arguably the top leader of our local beer industry, GreenBench is not only committed to the best tasting beer, they also focus on the best overall brewery experience. Located in the safe and walkable EDGE District, this casual and relaxed tasting room and huge open green space is a destination. Make a day out of drinking at GreenBench, eating at the nearby Mercado (Mexican food) or Bodega (Latin food), check out the new and modern event space, Webb's City Cellar, an ideal venue for larger parties.

Cage

With aliens painted on the wall and the sometimes very loud live bands, this place has a knack for drama. If you're in the mood to hang with some high quality and great tasting beer, you might want to check it out. Large open spaces make this a great location for kiddos to run around during the day.

3 Daughters

Always lively, the family friendly vibe here is a local favorite. Families flock here because they know about the games and tasty food offered by the rotating food trucks that keep the kiddos and parents happy. The Beach Blonde Pale Ale, The Strawberry Sour, and the Raspberry Hard Seltzer are always refreshing. Located in the Arts Warehouse District, you are a short walk to the cute gift shop at Creative Clay and The Bikery, a cute little bike and coffee shop where you can find the Honey Badger, one of my favorite cups of java in town, and Pinellas Ale Works.

Cycle

Some describe Cycle as loud and indie. I would tend to agree, but also enjoy the sours and pale ales that make this brewery a standout choice in DTSP. Known for their imperial stouts (tastes like dessert) and coffee beers, Cycle is a good choice for a group that likes to keep the party going after dinner. With beers named Cream and Sugar Please, it might be worth a try, right?

Avid Brewing Co.

Beer and hydroponic gardening are front and center stage at Avid Brewing Co. and both execute a strong performance. The ambiance is sleek, posh, and very popular with women. The 1830 Golden and the Reciprocal Plum Sour would win best lead actress at the Oscars if they had that kind of thing for beer.

With several dozen beer drinking options in St. Pete, it's not possible to list them all here. However, some other favorites include Flying Boat Brewing Company (think game night with a neighborhood vibe and fiercely competitive themed trivia nights), Ale and The Witch and The Independent. If you're still on the fence on whether or not to include a brewery in your itinerary, take note that some of these locations offer good wine choices as well as ciders and even hard seltzers. With tap lists and drink choices constantly changing, if you're not a beer drinker, it's best to contact the brewery to make sure that they are offering other choices than beer during your visit.

FESTIVALS AND EVENTS

SUNRISE SALE

If you happen to come in July during the week and are a morning person, there is one day a year when the shops open at sunrise (6:45 ish) and have the most incredible deals! I literally got a pair of jeans from Plain Jane this year that are regularly $110 for $15. Ok, so maybe I bought 2 pairs. But one was white and one had embroidered flowers, so how could I not get both? So many of the boutiques have mimosas and snacks, and it is so much fun! Some groups will come in pajamas and make a day of it, going for brunch afterwards. The city has been doing this for over 45 years, and I calendar the date as soon as they announce it!

MAINSAIL ART FESTIVAL

In April, St. Pete hosts an incredible art festival in Vinoy Park, along the waterfront in the heart of downtown. The festival is free, so even if you don't want to buy anything, it is so much fun to look! Although I am pretty sure for the right price, the artists will find a way to mail your purchase to you if that is a concern ;) There are some gorgeous, huge paintings and statues that cost thousands, but we also got some beautiful glass nightlights with animals on them for toddler birthday gifts, so there really is something for every taste and budget.

ART WALK

About 40 galleries and studios stay open late the second Saturday of every month and keep their doors open until 9:00 pm. There is a trolley you can ride with 20 stops near these galleries. There's a map online of the participating places and trolley stops, so if you happen to visit the second weekend of the month, this should definitely be on your list! It is the perfect way to feel the artistic vibe of the city and may even inspire you to take a class at the Morean Arts Center or The Clay Center.

JOHN'S PASS SEAFOOD FEST

If you're here in October during this event, you'll want to plan on taking a day trip to John's Pass in Madeira Beach so you can see what it looks like when our local seafood industry, musicians and hundreds of crafts vendors come together to put on an unforgettable event. You'll want to bring cash, your love for loud music and a huge appetite. If you're a Halloween lover, or simply put a premium on dressing up in a fun costume, take note of the very competitive and highly regarded adult costume contest.

FIRESTONE GRAND PRIX

St. Pete likes to live (and grow) in the fast lane. Every year in March they invite the best Indy Car drivers in the world to drive super-fast in circles around downtown to create what they say is the best motorsport event in the country. Bragging rights! I will warn you - if you are at all attached to your ability to hear, you might want to skip this event. Earmuffs are required for the people sitting in the first few rows. I used to live five miles outside of downtown and could hear the cars with the windows closed. However, if you are up for good food, drink and fast competition, you should check it out.

POPS IN THE PARK

Who doesn't need more free live classical music in their life? Under the stars. With a bottle of wine. With an amazing take out meal of your choice. Need I say more?! Once a year, on a Saturday night in October, The Florida Orchestra treats our ears to beautiful music in Vinoy Park. Other than takeout food and wine, all you need is a blanket and a willingness to relax outside by the waterfront.

GULFPORT ART WALK

We could do a whole chapter on the quaint town of Gulfport. It's en route to St. Pete Beach, so you should at least drive through to see all of the shops, restaurants and the rocking art scene. The Art Walk takes place on the First Friday and Third Saturday of every month, year-round. There are craft booths, and the local art shops and galleries stay open late for after-dinner shoppers. For Gulfport restaurants, we love Pia's Trattoria (not to be confused with Pia's Day Spa in the spas section).

Beaches

With over 35 miles of white sandy beaches that make the "Top Beaches in the US" list year after year, the only hard part about planning your trip to the beach is choosing which one and how to spend your time once you get there. From downtown you are approximately 20-30 minutes away from what many (correctly) consider the most desirable tourist destinations in the world. The information here is meant to be a starting point to help you plan your trip.

PASS-A-GRILLE BEACH/ST. PETE BEACH

These two neighboring communities are mostly residential with lots of public beach access, great choices for food and drink, and the iconic (and very pink) Don Cesar Hotel make this stretch of waterfront very popular. If your trip only permits one beach-going experience, Pass-A-Grille/St. Pete Beach is a safe choice. Take a dip in the pool at The Hotel Zamora while indulging in some mimosas, get pampered at Spa Oceana at The Don (the day pass is only $36 ladies!), and still have time for a quick shopping trip to the adorable 8th Avenue block where you will find clothing and souvenirs. Paradise Grill is a great place to catch the sunset with Grace and the very pricey (yet totally worth it) Maritana Grille at the Don Cesar, being good choices for a celebratory meal or vacay indulgence. Just a couple miles down the road is La Casa Del Pane, an Italian bakery gem. Perfect for grabbing a cafe con leche and homemade croissant for your beach stroll.

FORT DE SOTO PARK

In addition to the famous Fort De Soto that is a must see if you travel here, bike and kayak rentals make this beach and park a popular choice for adventure seekers who love being active outdoors. You can catch a ferry to Egmont Key and Shell Key, but check out the kid friendly concession stand before you make the trip. Right next to shelter 15, there is a great playground and the Fort De Soto Park Gift Shop is a great place to get a token of our natural wonders and they have a little something for everyone.

Redington Beach/ Indian Shores

Some locals note that there is limited beach access here and I tend to agree. However, the Salt Rock Grill is here and is one of my favorite restaurants of all time.

Madeira Beach

People love to shop and eat in John's Pass Village and Boardwalk or eat at the very popular Walt'z Fish Shak, where they serve the fish they catch that day and say "sorry guys" when they run out. Wave runners and jet skis are available for rental from Lady Godiva Fishing Charters. And grab a coffee at Addicted to the Bean on your way out.

Treasure Island

The very walkable and cottage like feel of Treasure Island is a great place to go for a long walk on the boardwalk, rent a bike or even partake in the huge inflatable slide into the Gulf of Mexico that all tourists seem to get a kick out of. For paddle board and kayak rentals and tours, check out Mad Beach Paddle Sports.

With so many options for activities, eating, drinking, and shopping, it can be overwhelming to create a beach trip itinerary. But don't worry. The trolley system, a safe and free (tips appreciated) option that goes up and down the entire stretch of beaches has you covered. If all you do here is stick your toes in the sand, you will still get a perfect glimpse into our beautiful and famous beaches.

ACTIVE OPTIONS

If breaking a sweat is on your itinerary while visiting the Burg, we're cheering you on AND we got you covered!

The Body Electric (The BE) is an excellent choice if you have time for only one yoga class. With top notch instructors who are committed to your zen, you'll be sure to feel mindful in your St. Pete surroundings after leaving this beautifully restored and very unique space. Take advantage of their private showers, and give yourself a bit of extra time before or after your class to peruse their gift shop.

SWEAT St. Pete is a popular training facility, where you can take a HIIT class in a group or private setting. Club Pilates is also an excellent choice for group or private fitness classes.

The Coast Bike Share program offers a bike rental option which has an hourly rate and requires downloading an app. For a completely tech free and off the grid alternative, you can check out Tony's Bike Shop located in the Grand Central District, one of the most vibrant areas of downtown, for all of your bike rental needs. If a leisurely ride through downtown doesn't fit the bill, the instructors at the well-trafficked Rush Cycle-St. Pete promises a fun and satisfying but intense spin class. Vertical Ventures is a great spot for those who understand that few things in life can offer happiness like a rock-climbing session. Indoors and safe.

We're not sure this qualifies as "active" but if you want to have a guiltless night (or day) of libation, check out the PedalPub St. Petersburg. The PedalPub brings the pub you bring the power of your pedal (by activating your legs) and together you will create the perfect workout activity!

Squeeze Juice Works and Karma Juice Bar & Eatery offer great options for clean and healthy eats after your workout. You can find the perfect bite of post workout bliss in the Cloud 9 Acai bowl at SoHo Juice Co. They also have chocolate cashew butter cups that are irresistible and delicious.

Family Time

Trolley Looper

This is a free trolley (tips for the driver appreciated) that makes (roughly) 30 minute loops around downtown. You can hop on and off, and kids love it! You get a little bit of St. Pete history but not too much, and it's a great way to get the lay of the land and scout out areas you want to explore.

Largo Train

If your little one likes trains and it happens to be the first weekend of the month, plan to venture a little outside of downtown to this ride-on train. Retired conductors have built and ride small trains around a 15-20 minute track. Plan to get there right when it opens at 9:00 or you'll be waiting in line for awhile. Thankfully there is a fantastic playground 30 feet from the train line.

Great Explorations/Sunken Gardens

About 5 minutes north of downtown by car is a kids' indoor (key for summer heat or rainy days) interactive museum. Local businesses sponsor the exhibits, and they are educational and fun. For example, the SPCA Tampa Bay has a mini vet center in Great Explorations where kids can learn about animals and how to care for them. Bella Brava has a pretend pizza making station, and Publix has a miniature grocery store complete with carts and registers. Just outside is Sunken Gardens, which is a walking trail through gardens with wildlife. It's not like a zoo, so set realistic expectations with the littles, but there are some beautiful birds, and it is super zen for the parents after the not-so-zen Great Explorations inside.

Pinellas Trail

My favorite trail ride starts downtown at Craft Kafé, where you can pick up the bike path at 1st Avenue S, ride west toward the Trop, the home of our Tampa Bay Rays. Starting at 22nd Street you can explore the Warehouse Arts District. Some fun and family friendly favorites to stop for bites and brews include Kazuba Distillery, 3 Daughters Brewery, The Bikery, and Creative Clay. If you are in for more exercise keep heading west, but be forewarned that there is not much to see until you reach Dunedin which is a legit trek.

CENTRAL ARTS DISTRICT WALKING MURAL TOUR

One of my favorite things about St. Pete is all the amazing street art. Leaving from the Florida CraftArt Gallery (see Florida CraftArt in the Shopping section), tours of impressive street art and murals run every Saturday from 10:00-11:30 am. At $19 for adults, $11 for children and zero dollars for kiddos under 5, this is an affordable activity that gives back to support local artists. If you are visiting mid-week, don't hesitate to call and request a private tour. Reservations are a must. If you're short on time and need an abbreviated DIY version of our street art, walk the alleyway between Central and 1st Ave North, starting at 3rd Street and head West. One standout mural that I swoon over every time is "All You Need Is Love" located at 299 Dr. Martin Luther King Jr. Boulevard N, facing 3rd Avenue If you happen to be here in October, make sure to attend the SHINE Mural Festival, one of the coolest events in the city.

THE PIER

While there has always been a Pier for Sunshine City tourists to enjoy (since the 1800s), the consensus among locals is the newest version is the crème de la crème, the best Pier the city has ever had. When you first arrive, you are greeted by the Marketplace, a great place to shop local, and the Bending Arc, a famous sculpture made out of nets. A traveling parent's dream; the Pier is the holy grail for easy and convenient family fun. Playgrounds for kids of all ages, a splash pad, local shopping, and art are all anchored by a snack bar that sells ice cream, pizza, wine, and beer. Wear the kids out before petting some sea creatures at the Tampa Bay Watch Discovery Center or eating at any of the restaurants that range from fine dining to a snack bar. With vast and beautiful green spaces with ocean views and Florida's finest flora and fauna, the Pier makes a perfect backdrop for any outdoor picnic you can imagine during your trip.

Note: We swear by (and owe many coffees to the moms who compile) www.sunshinecitykids.com. It is the calendar by which many local moms plan our weekends. If you are coming to St. Pete with littles, Check. It. Out.

MELANIE BOWMAN

Although she was born in St. Louis, Melanie considers herself a native Floridian having lived in Tampa Bay for over three decades. As a licensed clinical social worker and public health professional, Melanie is able to feel just as comfortable volunteering at her daughter's preschool as she does providing therapy to seniors in a nursing home. When she's not nerding out on all things books, you may find her cooking, hosting a dinner party for friends and family, bike riding, traveling, volunteering, or exploring St. Pete. Her favorite thing to do is the simplest and most important, spending time with her husband Jonathan and their two daughters Julia and Leah.

MELANIE'S IDEAL DAY

COFFEE ON THE VERANDAH AT THE VINOY
BREAKFAST AT THE SATURDAY MORNING
MARKET
WALK ALONG THE WATERFRONT
THE DALI MUSEUM
PICK UP LUNCH AT BODEGA AND BRING
IT ACROSS THE STREET TO GREEN BENCH
FOR A BEER OR CIDER
VISIT THE MURALS ON WAY TO THE
CHIHULY COLLECTION
CHIHULY COLLECTION (QUICK TRIP,
SMALL MUSEUM)
IL RITORNO FOR DINNER
NIGHT CAP AT THE CANOPY OR GELATO
AT PACIUGO FOR DESSERT.

MEREDITH GAUNCE

Although she grew up in Savannah (hence her first publication: Traveling Savannah: A Girls' Guide), Meredith moved to St. Pete in 2010 and will likely never leave. A lawyer by day, jewelry-maker by night, and a mom and wife all the time, Meredith loves taking advantage of all her home city has to offer. She loves animals and lives with her husband Andy, son Noah (5), and dogs Rudy and Penny (both 10ish). She treasures her girlfriends (I am looking at you, Erin and Mel!) and hopes this book inspires more girls' trips, spa days, happy hours and brunches.

MEREDITH'S IDEAL DAY
SATURDAY MORNING MARKET FOR COFFEE AND PERUSING
WOODHOUSE SPA FOR SOME PAMPERING
CASSIS FOR BRUNCH
SHOPPING AT: MISRED, ASHE COUTURE & PLAIN JANE
BRICK AND MORTAR FOR DINNER
HYPPO OR SWAH-REY FOR DESSERT

ERIN SALZER HANNA

Erin Salzer Hanna holds a Bachelor of Fine Arts from Carnegie Mellon University and a Masters of Landscape Architecture from the University of Pennsylvania. She currently practices in the fields of landscape design, graphic design, and illustration. She lives in Huntsville, Alabama with her husband Jesse, sons Henry and Charlie and 2 crazy cats.

CPSIA information can be obtained
at www.ICGtesting.com
Printed in the USA
LVHW071956180223
739828LV00011B/397